The Thoughts of a Young Man with an Old, Weary Soul

Gavin Lee

ISBN 978-1-7339406-0-3 (Paperback Edition)

ISBN 978-1-7339406-1-0 (Ebook Edition)

Library of Congress Control Number: 2019904191

Illustrations by Luke Hruska and Joan Wild.

Cover design by Joan Wild.

Printed in the United States of America

First printing April 2019

Published by Gavin Lee

3450 31st Drive

Everett, Washington, USA 98201

gslpoetry@gmail.com

For Brooke, who helped me when I most needed it.

<u>Acknowledgements</u>

I'd always thought of myself as a poet, but I never thought I was good enough to be taken seriously and publish a book until a few short months ago. I'm a man who's had a head filled with thoughts, and self-doubt is certainly one of the foremost. This collection is composed of both poems I wrote in high school and more recent poems, but all contain insight into the thoughts and ideas that have been swimming within my head, as well as something more. These poems were originally a way for me to get these feelings out on paper, but until recently I didn't think they were worth sharing for a variety of reasons. With this in mind, I think it's important that I thank a few people.

I'd first like to thank Brooke Hine for giving me the support I needed and helping me through some longstanding personal issues. Brooke, I don't think I'd be here now to create and share this collection with others were it not for you. You helped me realize I needed to start working through these issues instead of letting them go on. Things always get worse before they get better, though, and they certainly did get worse. Despite that, you were there for me when I needed it most, and this book would not exist without you. You've done so much for me; I don't think I'll ever be able to thank you enough, but I shall do my best.

I'd also like to thank my editor Kallie Falandays for helping this collection reach its greatest potential. This collection has a lot of heavy topics and I have a specific vision for it, yet you were able to work with that and push my writing to be the best it could be, and I thank you for that. I'd also like to thank Luke Hruska and Joan Wild for being some of the best friends I could ever ask for and helping me work through and design this collection. You've both done a great job helping shape this collection into what I had envisioned, and for that you have my thanks.

Lastly, I'd like to thank you, the reader, for having enough interest to read this book. I've been a sheltered person all my life and have always been afraid of putting myself out there, believing that no one would be interested in what I have to say. I've been even more afraid of sharing some of the struggles I've gone through, for one reason or another. But this is something I think is worth sharing, so thank you for giving me a chance.

Contents

Preface

Thought

Thoughts come into the mind

in tides and waves.

Sometimes they soothe the mind

and sometimes they send it into turmoil.

Thoughts of happiness

and joy and humor

wash up on the shore,

carried by the fluid-like surf.

But these thoughts don't stay.

They're carried back out to sea

and replaced by tsunamis of pain,

hurricanes of grief.

When these thoughts become

a crushing weight,

hope always radiates light,

piercing through blackened clouds.

And as time goes by,

thoughts of the

beloved One may

drift upon calm waves

and upon smooth sands.

Though one may wish for

such thoughts to last,

eventually other thoughts

that invoke happiness or pain

wash up on shore.

And so thought moves,

fluidly and elegantly,

calmly at times,

and violently at others.

I.   The Voices

Episode

It begins with the voices
rising,
whisper to scream,
all spouting vitriol,
trying to send the mind
into a confused disarray.

The hands start to tremble,
slowly reaching up
to press against the head,
grasping at a creased forehead
that hides the battle within.

A silent scream builds
as voices attack the gentle boy
behind the anguished face.

The legs begin to give way,
the body collapses to its knees
as tears well up
and stream down a strained face.

The voices don't stop,
screaming and shouting,
until the mind spirals into
an unstructured void.

The thoughts within,
once fluid as water,
become choppy, disjointed,
as if pumped through a kinked hose,
flowing out in painful intervals.

The hands, shaking,
no longer cover the head;
they clutch at it,
nails digging into hair and scalp.

The body folds over,
head on the ground,
and the silent scream
building within
releases as a
pained, sorrowful wail.

The whole body now shakes,
and the voices laugh,
but soon they subside
as the gentle boy
regains some control.

He sits up, wipes the tears from his eyes,
and wishes he weren't so alone.

Voices

It starts with a whisper
in the back of the mind,
a low, rasping voice,
so faint yet so clear.

You weak little creature.
You're a failure and you know it.

More whispers join in;
some say dreadful things,
some babble madly,
giggle and laugh.

he-he-he Ha-Ha-Ha-Ha
Look at you. You're a fool, lost and alone.
They're not your friends. They'll betray you.
You're a freak, but you're our little freak.
Don't listen to them, listen to me!
ha-ha-ha he-he-Ha-Ha

Soon they grow louder,
hateful,
saying I am a failure,
a weak, useless boy.

he-he-he-he Ha-ho-Ha   HAHAHA
Betray them first! Betray them first!
Who would love you? You're weak!
You're useless! We had a goal and you failed!
Why are you afraid to look in the mirror?
LOOK AT ME!!!
HAHAHAHAHA   Ho-Ho-Ha-Ha He-ha-ha-ha

They know what to say
to hurt my spirit;
they laugh and say
I only cause harm.

She could never love you.
 You'll only hurt her.
  She'd never understand you.
We're the only ones who will.
 You're letting her go?   *Pathetic.*
  You're weak.   *Why listen to us?*
    HA-HA-HA
 Look at you, all you do is feel sorry for yourself.

The voices shout
over each other
from different places
inside my mind.

HA-HA-HA-HA
LET ME TALK LET ME TALK
YOU THINK THIS IS FUNNY?
LET ME OUT, I WANT TO COME OUT AND PLAY!
PUT ME IN CONTROL, I'M THE ONE
WHO HELPED MAKE ALL THE DECISIONS!
LOOK AT ME ALREADY!!!
HA-HA-HA-HA-HA-HA-HA-HA-HA-HA-HA-HA-HA

Beneath the maddening cackle,
buried under the hatred,
is my one true voice,
alone and afraid.

It longs for the day
that it will have my
mind to itself, a
quiet, empty meadow.

But they don't want that.
The voices resist,
they want to be free,
loosed upon the world.

Let us out! Let us out let us out let us out!
I'll do what you can't, I won't be such a failure.
We'd already be fixing this world if not for you!
You're a coward! LET ME OUT!!!

They may be silenced
for a time by pills
or through force of will,
but they're always there.

There's always a voice,
a growling whisper
longing to be free
to spread words of hate.

Hating Myself

He runs through the woods,
darting between trees
and hopping over gentle streams,
vaulting across rolling rivers:
a young boy
no longer innocent.

He searches for a
place to hide himself
away from all his pursuers,
afraid of what they will say
about his
pure, kind, and hopeful thoughts.

He dreams of a world
of peace and plenty
where all life lives in harmony,
but his shadowy hunters
only want
a dark world of ruin.

They always find him,
curled up in a ball,
tears streaming down his face.
Their eyes, filled with hatred,
pierce through him,
and they begin to speak.

They spew vitriol,
poisoning the boy's thoughts.
He's weak, a useless little thing
who will only ever fail,
pathetic,
never meant to be loved.

The boy, now sobbing,
screaming out in pain,
tries to push all of them away
and be free of their hatred
as they goad
him to die.

So he keeps running,
trying to escape,
but he's starting to believe them.
Maybe what they say is right.
Maybe he
is all of what they say.

Instead of hiding
inside the forest,
perhaps he should listen to them
and hide at the bottom of
a river.

Emptiness

There's an emptiness within me,
a slowly growing void
that longs to be filled
with a beloved other,
one whose gentle embrace
can wrap around the
expanding edges
and shrink down this
hungry vacuum.
The more it grows,

the more alone I am.
It was born of a lack of love,
of not being cared for,
as a boy became a young man
far sooner than he should have.

As he grew, so did the voices
inside of his head;
they blocked out what kind words
others may have said

and instead showed the boy
the darkness that enveloped the world.

The boy felt detached from his peers,

unloved by his family,

and thought he was meant

to be a discarded failure.

I am a young man now,

but the emptiness feels the same,

expanding to the edges   of my heart,

as I long for   that someone

who would warmly embrace   a failure who has lived

devoid   of   love.

The emptiness remains,

ever growing,

ever hungry,

eating away at me from within.

Apology

I am sorry to have changed,
to no longer be the positive, loving boy I once was.

I am sorry I wasn't loved
and that it has changed me for the worse.

I am sorry I failed my hopes
and that I am now devoid of all hope.

I am sorry I am afraid,
unable to control my fears.

I am sorry I can trust no one,
not even myself.

I am sorry I am alone,
isolated because of these emotions.

I am sorry for my sins,
for all the wrongs I have committed.

I am sorry for the pain I have caused,
however large or small it may be.

I am sorry for the blood on my hands,
both mine and another's.

I am sorry I hurt myself,
seduced by a knife's edge.

I am sorry I hurt others
with both words and fists.

I am sorry I hurt my sister,
for I can still see the blood on her face.

I am sorry to have been blinded
by the voices within me.

I am sorry to have failed you,
to have always been such a failure.

I am sorry I haven't done better,
and I don't know if I can do better.

I am sorry for everything;
death or forgiveness would be a mercy to me now.

Fear Not Death

Fear not Death, my boy,
for she welcomes you to a loving embrace,
the only one you'll ever know.

Fear not Death, my boy,
for she offers you the sweetest kiss of all
to bid you a final goodnight.

Fear not Death, my boy,
for she will take you to a bright shining light,
like a great beacon for the soul.

Fear not Death, my boy,
for she cares for you like no one ever has
and like no one ever will.

Fear not Death, my boy, for she rests in you.
You need only reach out and take hold of her loving hand.

II.   The Weary Soul

Sanity

It's all held together
by a single, thin cord.
It was once strong, but the years,
with their unceasing pain,
have worn it to frayed threads.

The cruel voices try to sever
the loosely held cord,
and set everything loose,
breaking countless dams
that hold back the flow of thought.

A kind, young boy tries
to grip the cord tightly,
but the voices just cut
at him instead.

How long, one must wonder,
until the cord finally snaps,
or until the voices grow tired,
if ever they will.

The Edge of a Knife

It lies
there, resting,
waiting for a final push.
Metal cold and ever sharp,
the edge of a knife
waits to be warmed.
It is not a weapon; it is a tool
whose power remains unknown.
It inflicts pain, yes, upon the one
whom the edge slices through
and on those who may care
about this poor, weary soul.
Yet it is said that
the edge of a knife
can offer a sweet release
and help wash away the pain.
Fear of hurting others
holds the hand in hesitation
from making that final push.
Still, the mind can't
help but wonder
what that release must feel like,
and if anyone really cares at all.
And so it lies there, resting;
the edge of a knife
waits for that final push.

All That I've Seen

All that I've seen:
the ideals of love,
the power of hope,
the potential of life.

All that I've seen:
the happy children,
smiles on their faces,
their pure innocence.

All that I've seen:
the faces of my friends,
their joy and sorrow,
their pleasure and pain.

All that I've seen:
Brooke's smiling face,
Cameron's hearty laughter,
Luke's triumphant cries.

All that I've seen:
the pain of others,
deaths of millions,
the fault of my kind.

All that I've seen:
the cruelty of humans,
the violence they cause,
a plague on the world.

All that I've seen:
a broken family,
mother and sister,
lost in their anger.

All that I've seen:
the choices I've made,
the pain I have caused,
the regrets I have.

All that I've seen:
a stranger in the mirror,
the blood on my hands,
the monster in my shadow.

All that I've seen:
an end to my life,
a great empty void,
potential escape.

All that I've seen:
the love of my dreams,
the daughter of my hopes,
the life I could have.

Despite all that I've seen,
and all the emotions these images bring,
all I see now,
I do not wish to see.

The Meadow by the Woods

Bury me in the meadow by the woods
where the mountains loom in the distance
and through the forest, a short walk away,
waves orange from a setting sun lap
against the vast ocean's smooth sandy shore.

Bury me in the meadow by the woods
where naught can be heard but chirping birds
and the scatter of leaves from prancing deer,
nothing but wind blowing through the trees
and the kiss of water in the distance.

Bury me in the meadow by the woods
where I may finally find my rest
and be left beneath the old elder tree,
where the sweet earth will reclaim my tired body
and renew the loving cycle of life.

Bury me in the meadow by the woods
where so few people ever travel.
Leave me no tombstone or other markings,
and let all memory of me fade,
forgotten in the meadow by the woods.

Falling

It seems I'm always falling,
hurtling through
murky clouds.
I might
slow down,
no one
around
to fall
after.

But I'll
find
another.

I'll try
to catch
them,
I'll strain
in the dark,
searching
for those who
emanate
certain
light.

28

It's a
warm light
that
radiates
kindness
and love,
like a
tender smile
asking to
be returned.

I've been
falling
alone
so
long;

I just want
to catch one,
hold them
with my
heart.
They'll
cling
to me,
and lower me softly
to the ground.

But it never happens;
the light ones
always slip
from my
grasp.

I don't know how long I have:

The ground is fast
approaching,
and it isn't
slowing
down.

A World of Darkness

He walks through a colorless world,
a world of darkness, sifting
the inky black,
searching for a light.

He knows not where he is going.
He knows not where to look.

He sees only lifeless dark bodies,
color-drained corpses,
and he's unsure whether or not
they had lights while alive.

Shadows shroud the forms hovering nearby;
he's too afraid to sift through their murky cloaks,
afraid he may find another black soul,
another with no light.

He's searched all his life;
he's seen glimmers of light
in the gloomy landscape,
but he's never been able to fully understand one.

Maybe it's because
he's lost his own light,
stripped away by voices
that haunt his every step.

The voices thrive in the darkness
and try to keep him from approaching
one of these lights, bombarding the
already lost soul with useless directions.

He fears time may be running out,
for the darkness creeps in around him,
ready to swallow him whole.

III. The Thoughts of a Young Man: The Sound of His Own Voice

Reflection

There once was a time when I would look
in the mirror and see my own reflection:
A young boy, filled with hope and kindness,
ready to spread joy to the world.

As time drew on, I became more
withdrawn, talking only to myself
as I stared at my reflection.

One day it talked back to me with
a cold, calculating, strong-willed voice
that lacked all of my caring heart.

I was taken aback at first,
but then I began to see my reflection
as the only one who understood me.

Our talks were productive at first;
we would spend time debating, looking
from the bleak past toward a hopeful future.

Soon the reflection began to urge
me to become more like him,
more cold, more uncaring.

He said to sever all attachments, that they would
only bring pain because others didn't understand
me, not like he always would.

He said it was strength
that would lead us to a bright future,
not weakness or failure.

I listened for a time, growing cold
like my reflection as the kindness in
my heart began screaming in pain.

It wasn't until too late that I realized
when I gazed in the mirror,
a horrid monster gazed back:
a once benign creature
darkened by thought.

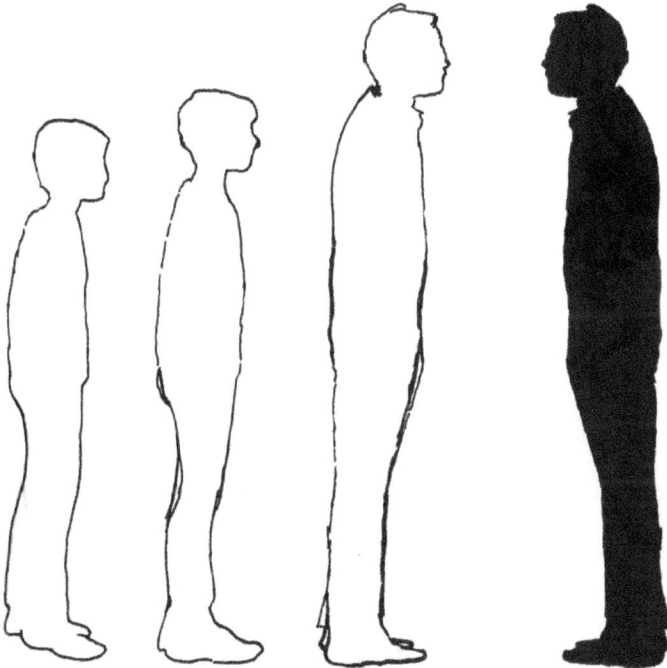

Fear

It bites at the mind, painfully
gnawing and creeping
into every decision.
This hungry, insidious creature
twists and warps every choice.
It is not just hate that is
the antithesis of love.
It is fear as well, a horrid parasite
that latches onto anything it can.
It wraps its hands around love,
choking it until it's consumed,
and all that's left is fear.
Hate is the offspring of fear,
for there cannot be hate without fear,
however small or subconscious
that hidden creature may be.
How can you hate another
if you aren't afraid of them,
afraid of what they can do?
How could a boy with a kind heart
hate humanity, his brothers and sisters,
if he wasn't made afraid of them
by the voices in his head?
If you aren't careful,
the parasite can control you, squirming
its way into your mind until
it possesses it entirely.
You must learn to conquer your fear,
lest you become absorbed by it,
as I have been.

Hope

Hope is like a sip of fine wine
and a deadly poison.
It can both create and destroy,
it can drive a person to greatness
or drive a person mad.
It managed to create a boy
who wanted to fix the world,
to make the world a haven
for life to flourish.
Then it crushed him
with the enormity of such a task,
fueling the voices within his head
as they showed him how blackened
the world really was.
Why the inherent duality? Why
must something so sweet
have the potential for such harm?
Much like wine, having too much
hope intoxicates the mind
and leads only to unobtainable
drunken wishes,
like those of a hopeful boy.
But to be devoid of hope
is to be devoid of
such a fine nectar.
A balance must be struck:
don't take too much,
like I once did,
and don't let it all leave your system,
as I now have.

Love

It drives all other emotions,
like a mother of many children
who nurtures some more than others,
cultivating a great garden
filled with unique flowers.
Many different kinds exist:
love of an object,
of a friend,
of a relative.
Yet what greater love can there ever be
than true love born of the heart,
beautiful like a flower in full bloom,
meant to be given to one special other,
one you can make smile a certain light,
one you can make laugh a melodious tune,
one you can share a warm embrace with
and feel safe in each other's arms.
It is when these flowers are exchanged
that the closest bond is made,
a bond that can soothe the mind's tumultuous thoughts.
These flowers have grown in me before,
yet they always seem to wilt
or simply be stillborn.
I hope one day I will grow,
so I may exchange flowers with another.
But for now, I am left alone
with not a flower to give,
having grown none of my own.

Trust

I let people latch their hooks onto me,
yet I attach no hooks of my own.
People place their faith in me,
and I guard it closely,
but I can't put my faith in them,
as fear keeps me from doing so:
fear of the pain people can cause,
and fear that the voices may be right,
that I only ever cause harm.
Now I am tangled up in lines,
as so many have needed me.
And it's been my pleasure
to be there for them
and to hold such a burden of bonds,
as it's all that I have left
to keep me attached to them.
I have yet to cast out my first hook
for someone else to catch.
Perhaps it's my fear of people,
or perhaps it's because I once tried
to latch myself to another,
and I only succeeded in pushing them away.
Or perhaps it's because I no longer
have a line to cast,
for it seems that I've lost the line
that's supposed to be hooked onto myself.

Adrift

I am adrift at sea,
my small boat old and weathered
with holes patched and leaks plugged
and naught but wind where a sail should be.

With my direction lost
and without a guiding force,
I'm at the sea's mercy,
hoping from the boat I won't be tossed.

Some days the sea is kind,
with clear skies and gentle waves,
and I repair my boat
with what strength and supplies I can find.

Other days it is cruel.
Howling winds and raging waves
batter my weary boat,
sending me back out, lost like a fool.

Sometimes waves carry me
to others in their own boats,
adrift in the ocean,
all damaged and lost to some degree.

Sometimes friendship is shown
when ideas and plans are shared,
and we repair our boats,
reminded that we are not alone.

But the sea does not care,
in time pushing us away,
back to empty ocean,
searching for others with but a prayer.

Rarely do I see land
where I might have sure footing
upon some solid ground, where
my boat might rest along the sand.

Such sights just never last,
and the waves again take me adrift,
stealing my hope, as I float
alone on the ocean vast.

Though I have no sail,
I search for another boat
to take along with mine and
find land to end my seaborne tale.

If I'm to steer a course,
I know I must make a sail,
but I don't know how,
and it's hard to try in the waves' force.

Perhaps another knows,
a kind soul with their own sail,
who can lend me a hand
until back out to sea my boat goes.

But the sea is callous,
and despite repairs I make,
my boat can't take much more before
it breaks in the ocean's malice.

And so my life shall be
at the mercy of the waves,
in my poor, weary boat,
I, with no rudder, adrift at sea.

About the Author

Originally from Bethel, Connecticut, Gavin Lee is a man with a passion for writing that rivals his passion for coffee. When he's not spaced out writing poetry, Gavin can be found trying to survive getting more degrees than he probably needs in aerospace engineering at WPI. His favorite pastimes include listening to music, hiking, writing, and trying to figure out how to take the word "hopeless" out of the self-prescribed term "hopeless romantic."

gslpoetry@gmail.com
facebook.com/GavinLeePoet
twitter: @GavinLeePoet

www.ingramcontent.com/pod-product-compliance
Lightning Source LLC
Chambersburg PA
CBHW022344040426
42449CB00006B/703